The Cost of Hate

The True Consequences of Systemic Islamophobia in Canada

Larisa Vedzizhev

All rights reserved. No part of this publication may be reproduced, distributed, or transmitted in any form or by any means, including photocopying, recording, or other electronic or mechanical methods without the publisher's prior written permission, except in the case of brief quotation embodied in critical reviews permitted by copyright law.

Table Of Content

Steps towards building a more just and inclusive Canada

Conclusion

The importance of recognizing the true cost of hate

A call to action for all Canadians.

Introduction

Systemic Islamophobia is a pervasive and institutionalized form of discrimination that affects Canadian Muslims on a daily basis. It is a problem because it perpetuates negative stereotypes and biases against Muslims, leading to discrimination, exclusion, and even violence. Systemic Islamophobia is not limited to a few individuals who hold prejudiced beliefs; it is embedded in the structures and institutions of Canadian society, such as the media, politics, and law enforcement.

Systemic Islamophobia affects the economic, social, and political opportunities available to Canadian Muslims. It limits their access to education, employment, and housing, and creates barriers to their participation in Canadian society. Moreover, it can have a significant psychological impact on individuals and communities, leading to feelings of isolation, fear, and anxiety.

The problem with systemic Islamophobia is not only that it harms Canadian Muslims, but it also undermines the fundamental values of Canadian democracy and human rights. Systemic Islamophobia goes against the Canadian Charter of Rights and Freedoms, which guarantees freedom of religion, equality, and non-discrimination. It also undermines Canada's reputation as a country that promotes diversity, inclusion, and social justice.

To address systemic Islamophobia, it is crucial to recognize its existence, understand its impact, and take action to challenge it. This requires a comprehensive and collaborative approach that involves individuals, communities, and government at all levels. Only by working together can Canadians build a more inclusive and equitable society, where all individuals can live without fear of discrimination and exclusion.

The goal of "The Cost of Hate: The True Consequences of Systemic Islamophobia in Canada" is to shed light on the devastating impact of systemic Islamophobia on Canadian Muslims and to inspire action to challenge it. By providing a comprehensive analysis of the economic, social, and political costs of discrimination and hate towards Muslims in Canada, the book aims to increase awareness of this pervasive problem and motivate readers to take concrete steps towards promoting inclusion and social justice.

The book seeks to challenge stereotypes and biases against Muslims by presenting the diverse experiences and perspectives of Canadian Muslims. Through personal stories, interviews, and statistical data, readers will gain a deeper understanding of the ways in which systemic Islamophobia affects individuals and communities in Canada.

Ultimately, the book aims to contribute to building a more just and inclusive society for all Canadians, where individuals are valued and respected regardless of their religion, ethnicity, or background. By highlighting the true cost of hate, the book calls on all Canadians to take responsibility for challenging systemic Islamophobia and creating a society where diversity and inclusion are celebrated and valued.

Chapter 1: The History of Islamophobia in Canada

Early examples of Islamophobia in Canadian history

Early examples of Islamophobia in Canadian history can be traced back to the late 19th and early 20th centuries when Muslim immigrants began arriving in Canada. While the Muslim population was relatively small at the time, there were instances of discrimination and prejudice against them. Here are a few notable examples:

1. Continuous Passage Act (1908): The Canadian government implemented this legislation, which required immigrants to arrive in Canada by a continuous

journey, without stopping in another country. The act specifically targeted immigrants from South Asia, including Muslims, effectively making it difficult for them to immigrate to Canada. This discriminatory policy reflected the prevailing xenophobic sentiments of the time.

2. Komagata Maru Incident (1914): The Komagata Maru was a ship carrying 376 passengers, mostly Sikh and Muslim immigrants from India, who intended to settle in Canada. However, the ship was denied entry and was forced to return to India. The incident symbolized the discriminatory immigration policies and anti-Asian

sentiments prevalent in Canada during that period.

3. Anti-Muslim sentiments during World War I: During World War I, there was a rise in anti-Muslim sentiment in Canada due to the involvement of the Ottoman Empire (an Islamic state) on the opposing side. This led to suspicion and discrimination against Muslim communities, including the harassment of Turkish, Arab, and other Muslim individuals.

4. Ontario Regulation 17 (1912): Although not explicitly targeting Muslims, this regulation restricted the teaching of any language other than English in Ontario schools. It had a

significant impact on Muslim communities, as it limited their ability to maintain their cultural and religious practices within educational institutions.

5. Immigration Act (1952): The Immigration Act of 1952 introduced new criteria for immigrants, including a point system that prioritized those from Western European countries. This policy favored white immigrants and effectively excluded those from non-Western countries, including many Muslim-majority countries.

6. 1970 October Crisis: In 1970, the Front de libération du Québec (FLQ) kidnapped British diplomat James

Cross and Quebec cabinet minister Pierre Laporte. The Quebec government declared a state of emergency, and the federal government deployed the military to Quebec. During this time, many Muslim immigrants were wrongfully targeted and detained due to their ethnic and religious backgrounds. The events of the October Crisis reflected a broader trend of racial profiling and discrimination against Muslim communities.

7. Anti-Muslim hate crimes (2001-present): The events of September 11, 2001, led to a surge in anti-Muslim sentiment and hate crimes in Canada. Since then, there have been

numerous instances of Islamophobia in Canada, including hate speech, vandalism of mosques, and violent attacks on Muslims. These incidents illustrate the ongoing impact of systemic Islamophobia in Canadian society.

These historical examples demonstrate that Islamophobia is not a new phenomenon in Canada. Instead, it is deeply rooted in Canadian history and reflects a broader pattern of discrimination and prejudice against immigrant communities. By understanding these historical instances, we can better understand the impact of systemic Islamophobia on Canadian Muslims today and work towards creating a more just and inclusive society for all.

The impact of 9/11 and the "War on Terror"

The events of 9/11 and the subsequent "War on Terror" had a profound impact on Canadian Muslims and contributed to the rise of systemic Islamophobia in Canada. Here are a few key ways in which 9/11 and the "War on Terror" have affected Canadian Muslims:

1. Increase in surveillance and racial profiling: Following 9/11, the Canadian government implemented a series of measures aimed at identifying and monitoring potential terrorist threats. This included increased surveillance

and profiling of Muslims, particularly those from countries deemed high-risk. These policies perpetuated stereotypes and contributed to the perception that all Muslims were potential terrorists.

2. Discriminatory immigration policies: In the years following 9/11, the Canadian government introduced a series of immigration policies that disproportionately affected Muslims. For example, the Safe Third Country Agreement, which requires refugee claimants to seek asylum in the first safe country they arrive in, effectively closed Canada's border to many Muslim refugees fleeing persecution.

3. Harassment and hate crimes: The events of 9/11 led to a surge in anti-Muslim sentiment in Canada, which in turn contributed to a rise in hate crimes and discrimination against Canadian Muslims. According to Statistics Canada, hate crimes targeting Muslims increased by 253% between 2012 and 2015.

4. Stigmatization and marginalization: The climate of fear and suspicion that emerged in the aftermath of 9/11 contributed to the stigmatization and marginalization of Canadian Muslims. Many felt compelled to hide their religious or cultural identities, while others were subjected to verbal abuse,

bullying, or discrimination in the workplace and educational settings.

5. Racial profiling and airport security measures: The events of 9/11 prompted significant changes in airport security protocols, leading to an increased focus on individuals who were perceived to fit the profile of a potential terrorist. As a result, Canadian Muslims, particularly those who wore visible religious attire such as hijabs or turbans, became targets of racial profiling at airports. They were subject to heightened scrutiny, additional screening, and unnecessary questioning, often based solely on their religious or ethnic appearance.

6. Erosion of civil liberties: In the name of national security and counterterrorism efforts, certain policies and legislation were introduced that eroded civil liberties and disproportionately affected Canadian Muslims. Examples include expanded surveillance powers, increased government access to personal information, and the passage of laws such as the Anti-Terrorism Act (Bill C-51). These measures raised concerns about privacy rights, freedom of expression, and due process, leading to a climate of mistrust and marginalization among Canadian Muslims.

7. Impact on mental health and well-being: The climate of Islamophobia fueled by the events of 9/11 and the "War on Terror" had a significant impact on the mental health and well-being of Canadian Muslims. The constant scrutiny, discrimination, and negative portrayal in media created a sense of fear, anxiety, and alienation. Studies have shown higher rates of stress, depression, and psychological distress among Canadian Muslims, highlighting the detrimental effects of systemic Islamophobia on their overall well-being.

8. Chilling effect on free expression and activism: The heightened surveillance and increased scrutiny of Muslim

communities following 9/11 created a chilling effect on free expression and activism. Many individuals within the community felt hesitant to voice their opinions, engage in political or social activism, or openly discuss issues related to Islamophobia or foreign policy, fearing potential repercussions or being labeled as sympathizers with terrorism.

The impact of 9/11 and the subsequent "War on Terror" on Canadian Muslims has been profound, leading to a climate of fear, discrimination, and marginalization. Recognizing and addressing these impacts is crucial to fostering a more inclusive and equitable society that respects the rights and dignity of all its citizens, irrespective of their religious or ethnic backgrounds.

The role of media and politics in perpetuating Islamophobic attitudes

The role of media and politics in perpetuating Islamophobic attitudes is significant and has contributed to the persistence of systemic Islamophobia in Canada. Here are some key aspects of their influence:

1. Misrepresentation and sensationalism: Media outlets have played a role in perpetuating Islamophobic attitudes through misrepresentation and sensationalism. Negative stereotypes and biased portrayals of Muslims and

Islam are often sensationalized, emphasizing stories that reinforce preconceived notions of Muslims as terrorists or threats to national security. This skewed representation creates a distorted view of the Muslim community and fosters fear and mistrust among the general public.

2. Islamophobic rhetoric in political discourse: Politicians have sometimes engaged in Islamophobic rhetoric, either directly or indirectly. This kind of rhetoric reinforces negative stereotypes, fuels public fears, and perpetuates the idea that Muslims are inherently dangerous or incompatible with Canadian values. Such political discourse not only legitimizes

Islamophobia but also sets the tone for discriminatory policies and actions.

3. Policy decisions targeting Muslims: Certain policies and actions by governments, influenced by Islamophobic narratives, have specifically targeted Muslims. Examples include discriminatory immigration policies, surveillance programs targeting Muslim communities, and the proposed bans on religious symbols, such as the niqab or hijab, in public spaces. These policies reinforce a sense of otherness and exclusion, further marginalizing Canadian Muslims.

4. Lack of diverse representation: Media and politics often lack diverse representation of Muslims and their perspectives. This underrepresentation reinforces the notion that Muslims are a monolithic group and fails to challenge stereotypes. When Muslim voices and experiences are absent or marginalized, it perpetuates a one-sided narrative that reinforces Islamophobia.

5. Amplification of extremist voices: Media coverage sometimes amplifies the voices of extremist individuals or groups, giving them a platform to disseminate their Islamophobic ideologies. This can contribute to the perception that such extreme views are more prevalent than they actually are,

and it further fuels stereotypes and fears.

Addressing the role of media and politics in perpetuating Islamophobic attitudes requires a commitment to responsible journalism, diverse representation, and political leadership that promotes inclusivity, tolerance, and respect for all communities. By challenging stereotypes, promoting accurate and balanced portrayals, and fostering dialogue, we can work towards a more informed and inclusive public discourse that counters Islamophobia.

Chapter 2: The Economic Costs of Systemic Islamophobia

Employment discrimination and its impact on Canadian Muslims

Employment discrimination refers to unfair treatment or barriers faced by individuals based on their race, religion, or other personal characteristics in the workplace. Canadian Muslims have reported experiencing employment discrimination in various forms, including:

1. Hiring bias: Canadian Muslims have reported facing barriers in securing employment due to discrimination during the hiring process. Some employers may consciously or

unconsciously discriminate against Muslim job candidates based on their religious affiliation or the perception that they may not fit into the company's culture or values.

2. Harassment and bullying: Muslim employees have reported experiencing harassment and bullying in the workplace due to their religious affiliation or cultural practices. This can range from comments or jokes based on stereotypes to more severe forms of harassment such as threats or physical violence.

3. Unequal treatment and opportunities: Canadian Muslims may experience unequal treatment and opportunities in

the workplace. This can include being denied promotions or leadership roles, being paid less than their non-Muslim counterparts, or being excluded from certain opportunities due to their religion.

The impact of employment discrimination on Canadian Muslims can be significant. Discrimination can lead to lower job satisfaction, increased stress and anxiety, and reduced productivity. It can also result in economic disadvantage and limit career opportunities, leading to a wider impact on the financial well-being and social mobility of Muslim individuals and their families.

Moreover, employment discrimination against Canadian Muslims has long-term consequences for their professional growth and advancement. When qualified individuals are denied opportunities or face obstacles solely based on their religious identity, it hinders their ability to fully utilize their skills and contribute to their chosen fields. This not only limits their potential for career progression but also deprives Canadian society of the diverse perspectives, talents, and contributions that they bring.

The impact of employment discrimination on Canadian Muslims extends beyond the individual level and affects the broader community. Discrimination in the workplace sends a message that Muslims are not valued or fully accepted as equal members of society. It creates a climate of exclusion and can contribute to feelings of marginalization and alienation. This, in turn, can have detrimental effects on social cohesion, interfaith relations, and the overall fabric of Canadian society.

Furthermore, employment discrimination against Canadian Muslims perpetuates systemic Islamophobia. When discriminatory practices are normalized or overlooked, it reinforces the notion that Muslims are somehow less deserving of fair treatment and opportunities. It contributes to the negative stereotypes and biases that fuel broader societal prejudices and discrimination against Muslims. This not only impacts individuals' employment prospects but also their overall well-being, sense of belonging, and perception of their place within Canadian society.

Employment discrimination can also have broader implications for Canadian society. Discrimination based on religion, race, or ethnicity undermines Canada's commitment to diversity and inclusivity, eroding trust in institutions and social cohesion. It reinforces negative stereotypes and fuels prejudice and intolerance, which can contribute to the perpetuation of systemic Islamophobia. Addressing employment discrimination and promoting equal opportunities for Canadian Muslims is not only a matter of individual rights but also a necessary step towards building a more inclusive and equitable society for all.

The cost of anti-Muslim hate crimes

Anti-Muslim hate crimes impose significant costs on individuals, communities, and society as a whole. Here are some of the costs associated with anti-Muslim hate crimes:

1. Physical and psychological harm: Hate crimes can cause direct physical injuries and emotional trauma to the victims. The physical injuries may require medical attention, resulting in healthcare costs. The psychological impact can be long-lasting, leading to anxiety, depression, post-traumatic stress disorder (PTSD), and a decreased sense of security and well-being.

2. Economic impact on individuals: Victims of hate crimes may face financial burdens, including medical expenses, loss of income due to physical or emotional injuries, and potential property damage. These economic consequences can lead to financial instability and hardship for individuals and their families.

3. Community cohesion and social integration: Hate crimes create a climate of fear and hostility within affected communities. They can erode trust and social cohesion, making it more challenging for community members to feel safe and fully participate in society. This hampers social integration and prevents the

realization of a truly inclusive and multicultural society.

4. Cost of law enforcement and criminal justice system: Hate crimes require investigations, law enforcement resources, and legal proceedings. These costs are borne by taxpayers and can place an additional burden on an already strained criminal justice system.

5. Impact on social fabric and intergroup relations: Anti-Muslim hate crimes contribute to the fragmentation of society, breeding mistrust and animosity between different religious and ethnic groups. They undermine

efforts to foster interfaith dialogue, multiculturalism, and social harmony.

6. Diminished economic productivity: Hate crimes can negatively affect the overall economic productivity of a community or region. They create an atmosphere of fear and insecurity, which can deter investment, tourism, and business development. In addition, individuals who are targets of hate crimes may face barriers to accessing employment, education, or housing, limiting their economic opportunities and potential contributions to the economy.

7. Long-term consequences: The impact of anti-Muslim hate crimes extends

beyond the immediate aftermath. It can have lasting effects on individuals' perceptions, sense of safety, and trust in institutions. This can perpetuate a cycle of discrimination, exclusion, and marginalization for affected individuals and communities.

Addressing the cost of anti-Muslim hate crimes requires comprehensive efforts to prevent, report, and effectively respond to hate crimes. This includes implementing robust hate crime legislation, raising awareness, fostering intergroup dialogue, promoting diversity and inclusion, and providing support services to victims. By addressing the root causes of Islamophobia and hate crimes, society can work towards creating a safer, more inclusive environment for all individuals, regardless of their religious background.

The economic potential lost due to Islamophobic policies and attitudes

Islamophobic policies and attitudes have significant economic consequences that are often overlooked. Here are some of the ways in which Islamophobia can result in lost economic potential:

1. Discrimination in employment: Discrimination against Muslims in hiring practices and workplace promotions can lead to a loss of talented and skilled individuals in the workforce. This limits the potential of

companies and organizations to benefit from a diverse range of perspectives and expertise.

2. Reduced economic participation: Islamophobia can create a climate of fear and exclusion, which can discourage Muslims from participating fully in economic activities such as entrepreneurship and business development. This reduces the economic potential of affected individuals and communities, resulting in lost opportunities for innovation, growth, and job creation.

3. Negative impact on tourism: Islamophobic policies and attitudes can also have a negative impact on the

tourism industry. If tourists perceive a destination to be hostile or unwelcoming to Muslims, they may choose to visit other destinations, resulting in lost revenue for businesses and communities that rely on tourism.

4. Reduced foreign investment: Discriminatory policies and attitudes can also deter foreign investors who may view a country or region as unwelcoming or hostile. This can limit the potential for economic growth and development, as foreign investment is often a significant source of capital for many industries.

5. Increased economic costs: Islamophobic policies can result in

additional economic costs, such as increased security measures, heightened surveillance, and legal expenses. These costs are often borne by taxpayers and can divert resources away from more productive uses.

6. Lost productivity and innovation: When talented and skilled individuals are excluded or discriminated against, it results in lost productivity and innovation potential. This limits the economic potential of the affected individuals and society as a whole.

Addressing the economic potential lost due to Islamophobic policies and attitudes requires a multi-faceted approach. This includes implementing inclusive policies and practices, promoting diversity and inclusion in all aspects of society, and raising awareness about the economic benefits of diversity. By doing so, society can realize the full potential of all individuals, regardless of their religious background, resulting in a more prosperous and inclusive future.

Chapter 3: The Social Costs of Systemic Islamophobia

The psychological impact of Islamophobia on Canadian Muslims

Islamophobia has significant psychological impacts on Canadian Muslims, affecting their mental health, well-being, and sense of belonging. Here are some key aspects of the psychological impact of Islamophobia:

1. Anxiety and fear: Canadian Muslims often experience heightened levels of anxiety and fear due to Islamophobic attitudes and actions. The constant threat of discrimination, hate crimes, or verbal abuse creates a pervasive sense of insecurity and unease, impacting

their daily lives and overall sense of safety.

2. Identity and self-esteem: Islamophobia can lead to feelings of self-doubt and diminished self-esteem among Canadian Muslims. The negative portrayal of Islam and Muslims in media and society can make individuals question their own identity and sense of belonging, leading to a sense of internal conflict and confusion.

3. Stigmatization and marginalization: Islamophobic attitudes and actions contribute to the stigmatization and marginalization of Canadian Muslims. This can lead to feelings of exclusion, isolation, and a sense of being

"othered" within their own society. It erodes their sense of belonging and can have detrimental effects on their mental well-being.

4. Psychological distress: Experiencing Islamophobia can result in psychological distress, including symptoms of depression, anxiety disorders, post-traumatic stress disorder (PTSD), and other mental health challenges. The cumulative effects of discrimination, microaggressions, and systemic bias can take a toll on individuals' emotional and psychological well-being.

5. Impact on relationships and social connections: Islamophobia can strain

relationships and social connections for Canadian Muslims. It may lead to strained interactions with peers, colleagues, or even family members who hold prejudiced views. The fear of discrimination can also lead to social withdrawal and isolation, affecting their support networks and sense of community.

6. Internalized Islamophobia: Some Canadian Muslims may internalize Islamophobic attitudes and stereotypes, leading to self-blame or feelings of shame about their own religious identity. Internalized Islamophobia can further exacerbate psychological distress and hinder individuals from

fully embracing their faith and cultural heritage.

Addressing the psychological impact of Islamophobia requires a multifaceted approach. It involves creating safe spaces for individuals to express their experiences, providing culturally sensitive mental health support services, promoting education and awareness to challenge stereotypes, and fostering inclusive environments that value diversity and promote social cohesion. By addressing the psychological well-being of Canadian Muslims, society can work towards a more inclusive and supportive environment for all individuals, irrespective of their religious background.

The social exclusion of Muslim communities

Social exclusion of Muslim communities in Canada is a significant issue that results in many negative impacts on individuals, families, and communities. Social exclusion can manifest in various forms, including discrimination, stigmatization, and marginalization, and it can take a toll on individuals' sense of identity, belonging, and self-worth.

Here are some key aspects of the social exclusion of Muslim communities in Canada:

1. Employment: Muslim individuals often face barriers to employment due to

discrimination, lack of accommodation, and bias in the hiring process. This can lead to economic hardship, lower social status, and a sense of exclusion from mainstream society.

2. Education: Muslim children and youth may experience bullying, prejudice, and discrimination in schools, leading to lower academic achievement and higher dropout rates. This can result in a lack of opportunities and decreased social mobility, further exacerbating social exclusion.

3. Housing: Muslim individuals and families may face discrimination in the housing market, leading to limited access to affordable and safe housing.

This can result in overcrowding, substandard living conditions, and instability, further increasing their sense of social exclusion.

4. Political participation: Muslim communities may feel excluded from the political process due to discriminatory policies or lack of representation in decision-making processes. This can lead to a sense of powerlessness and disengagement from the larger society.

5. Cultural and social practices: Muslim communities may experience exclusion and discrimination due to their cultural and religious practices, such as wearing the hijab or participating in religious

events. This can result in a sense of alienation and marginalization from mainstream society.

6. Community cohesion: Social exclusion can lead to a breakdown in community cohesion and social capital, making it more challenging for individuals to access resources, support, and social networks. This can further exacerbate feelings of isolation and exclusion.

Addressing the social exclusion of Muslim communities requires a multifaceted approach, including efforts to combat discrimination and bias, promote diversity and inclusion, and create opportunities for economic and social mobility. Providing support for community-led initiatives, fostering intercultural understanding and dialogue, and promoting policies that address systemic barriers to inclusion can all help reduce the social exclusion experienced by Muslim communities.

The impact of increased surveillance and racial profiling

Increased surveillance and racial profiling have a profound impact on individuals and communities, particularly those from Muslim backgrounds. Here are some key aspects of their impact:

1. Erosion of trust: Surveillance and racial profiling create a climate of suspicion and mistrust between communities and

law enforcement agencies. When individuals are targeted based on their perceived religious or ethnic background rather than their actual behavior or actions, it undermines trust and cooperation with authorities, hindering efforts to build safe and inclusive communities.

2. Psychological distress: Constant surveillance and the fear of being racially profiled can lead to significant psychological distress among individuals. It creates a sense of being constantly watched, judged, or treated as potential threats solely based on their religious or ethnic identity. This can contribute to anxiety, stress, and a

diminished sense of security and well-being.

3. Stigmatization and marginalization: Increased surveillance and racial profiling contribute to the stigmatization and marginalization of Muslim communities. It reinforces negative stereotypes, perpetuates biases, and labels individuals as suspect or inherently dangerous based on their religious or ethnic identity. This can lead to social exclusion, isolation, and a sense of not fully belonging within society.

4. Impact on community cohesion: Surveillance and racial profiling can fracture community cohesion and trust

within Muslim communities. The fear and distrust created by such practices can lead to self-imposed isolation, limited social interactions, and a reluctance to engage with others outside their immediate circles. This hampers community building and integration, hindering social cohesion and shared understanding.

5. Inhibition of freedom and expression: Increased surveillance and racial profiling may lead individuals to curtail their freedom of expression and cultural practices out of fear of being targeted or perceived as threats. This undermines individuals' ability to fully exercise their rights and participate in society, restricting their freedom of

religion, speech, and cultural expression.

6. Reinforcement of systemic discrimination: Increased surveillance and racial profiling reinforce systemic discrimination against Muslim communities. It perpetuates the notion that Muslims are inherently suspicious or prone to extremism, perpetuating biases and fueling Islamophobia. This undermines efforts to create a society that values diversity, equality, and respect for all.

Efforts to address increased surveillance and racial profiling must prioritize the protection of civil liberties, respect for human rights, and the need for effective and non-discriminatory policing practices. This includes ensuring that law enforcement agencies are held accountable for discriminatory practices and implementing measures to promote diversity, inclusion, and cultural understanding. It is also essential to engage with affected communities to understand their experiences, needs, and priorities and to foster a sense of trust and collaboration between these communities and law enforcement agencies.

Chapter 4: The Political Costs of Systemic Islamophobia

The effect of Islamophobia on Canadian democracy

Islamophobia can have a significant impact on Canadian democracy, undermining the principles of equality, fairness, and justice that are essential for a healthy and functioning democratic society. Here are some ways in which Islamophobia can affect Canadian democracy:

1. Discrimination and exclusion: Islamophobia can perpetuate discriminatory attitudes and practices that exclude Muslims from fully participating in Canadian society. This

can limit the representation of diverse perspectives in the political sphere, leading to a lack of diversity in decision-making processes and policies.

2. Divisiveness and polarization: Islamophobic rhetoric and policies can create divisions within Canadian society, pitting different communities against each other and fostering a sense of "us vs. them." This can erode social cohesion, reduce trust in democratic institutions, and undermine efforts to build a more inclusive and equitable society.

3. Limiting freedom of expression: Islamophobia can lead to censorship

and the suppression of freedom of expression, particularly for Muslims who may face retaliation or backlash for expressing their views. This can limit the diversity of perspectives in public discourse, further reinforcing the marginalization of Muslim voices in Canadian society.

4. Undermining human rights: Islamophobia can also undermine human rights protections, particularly for Canadian Muslims who may face discriminatory treatment in areas such as employment, education, housing, and access to public services. This can limit their ability to fully exercise their rights as Canadian citizens, further

reinforcing feelings of exclusion and marginalization.

5. Damaging Canada's international reputation: Canada's reputation as a tolerant and inclusive society can be undermined by the presence of Islamophobia, particularly on the global stage. This can harm Canada's relationships with other countries and limit its ability to promote human rights and democracy internationally.

To combat the impact of Islamophobia on Canadian democracy, it is essential to promote inclusive and equitable policies and practices that recognize the contributions and diversity of all Canadians, including those who identify as Muslim. This includes increasing representation of diverse perspectives in political decision-making processes, protecting freedom of expression, combating discrimination, and promoting human rights protections for all Canadians. It is also important to engage in dialogue and education to foster understanding and promote respectful communication across diverse communities. By working together to address Islamophobia, Canadians can build a stronger and more resilient democracy that values diversity, inclusion, and justice.

The impact of Islamophobic policies on Canadian foreign relations

Islamophobic policies in Canada can have a significant impact on Canadian foreign relations, straining diplomatic relationships and undermining Canada's global reputation. Here are some key impacts of Islamophobic policies on Canadian foreign relations:

Perception of intolerance: Islamophobic policies can create a perception that Canada is an intolerant country that discriminates against Muslims. This can damage Canada's reputation as a diverse and inclusive nation, eroding trust and goodwill with other countries, particularly those with large Muslim populations.

Human rights concerns: Islamophobic policies can raise human rights concerns among the international community. Such policies are viewed as discriminatory and contrary to principles of equality, freedom of religion, and non-discrimination. This can result in criticism and condemnation from other countries and international organizations, straining diplomatic relations.

Trade and economic repercussions: Islamophobic policies can have negative economic consequences. Countries may respond by imposing trade restrictions, reducing investments, or boycotting Canadian products or services. This can harm Canada's economic interests and disrupt trade relations, affecting industries and businesses that rely on international partnerships.

Weakening global influence: Canada's stance on Islamophobia can impact its ability to exert influence and advocate for human rights and democratic values on the global stage. Countries may be less inclined to collaborate with Canada or seek its leadership on human rights issues if they perceive a disconnect between its domestic policies and its international commitments.

Collaboration on security and counter-terrorism: Effective collaboration on security and counter-terrorism efforts requires trust and cooperation with Muslim-majority countries. Islamophobic policies can hinder cooperation by undermining trust, increasing suspicion, and reinforcing negative stereotypes. This can impede information sharing and hinder joint efforts to combat terrorism and extremism.

Diminished soft power: Canada's soft power, which relies on its reputation for inclusivity, diversity, and respect for human rights, can be diminished by Islamophobic policies. This can impact its ability to influence international opinion, build coalitions, and promote its values and interests in global forums.

Addressing the impact of Islamophobic policies on Canadian foreign relations requires a commitment to upholding human rights, promoting inclusivity, and addressing discriminatory policies. Canada can rebuild trust and strengthen its global reputation by demonstrating a genuine commitment to diversity, inclusivity, and respect for human rights at home and abroad. Engaging in dialogue, fostering understanding, and promoting cooperation with Muslim-majority countries are crucial steps towards repairing relationships and reestablishing Canada's position as a leader in promoting peace, tolerance, and human rights.

The role of government in challenging Islamophobia and promoting inclusion

The Canadian government has a key role to play in challenging Islamophobia and promoting inclusion. Here are some key ways that the government can work towards this:

1. Education and awareness: The government can develop education and awareness programs to promote understanding and combat misinformation about Islam and Muslims. This can include programs

for schools, workplaces, and communities, as well as initiatives to train government employees on diversity and inclusion.

2. Legislation and policies: The government can enact legislation and policies to address discrimination and promote inclusion. This can include anti-discrimination laws, policies that promote diversity and inclusion in hiring and promotion, and measures to ensure equal access to public services and programs.

3. Consultation with Muslim communities: The government can consult with Muslim communities to better understand their experiences and

needs, and to involve them in developing policies and programs that address discrimination and promote inclusion.

4. Representation and participation: The government can work to increase representation and participation of Muslims in decision-making processes and public life. This can include appointing Muslims to positions of leadership and authority, as well as ensuring that Muslim voices are heard in policy development and community consultations.

5. Addressing systemic issues: The government can work to address systemic issues that contribute to

Islamophobia, such as poverty, unemployment, and social exclusion. This can include initiatives to improve access to education, employment, and housing, as well as measures to address inequalities in the justice system and other institutions.

6. Condemning hate speech and hate crimes: The government can take a strong stance against hate speech and hate crimes, and work to prosecute those who engage in such activities. This can include partnering with law enforcement agencies and community groups to prevent and address hate crimes, as well as supporting initiatives that promote tolerance and respect.

By taking proactive measures to address Islamophobia and promote inclusion, the Canadian government can help to create a more equitable and just society, and contribute to a more peaceful and prosperous world.

Chapter 5: Canadian Muslim Voices

Personal stories of discrimination and resilience

Personal stories of discrimination and resilience provide powerful insights into the lived experiences of individuals who have faced Islamophobia in Canada. These stories highlight the challenges and struggles faced by Canadian Muslims, as well as their resilience and determination to overcome adversity. Here are a few examples:

1. Sara's Story: Sara, a young Muslim woman, shares her experience of facing discrimination in the workplace. Despite being highly qualified and

skilled, Sara was repeatedly overlooked for promotions and faced microaggressions from colleagues. She recounts the emotional toll it took on her, but also emphasizes her resilience and determination to pursue her goals. Sara walks into her workplace every day, putting on a brave face despite the constant microaggressions she faces from her colleagues. Despite being highly qualified and skilled, she is repeatedly overlooked for promotions and excluded from important decision-making processes. She feels her confidence and self-worth slowly eroding away, but she refuses to let Islamophobia define her. With the support of her community and mentors, Sara networks and actively seeks out better opportunities. She finally finds a workplace that values her skills and provides a supportive environment, where she can thrive and be herself without fear of discrimination. Through networking and support from her community, Sara eventually found a workplace that valued her skills and provided a supportive environment.

2. Ahmed's Journey: Ahmed, a Canadian Muslim immigrant, shares his journey of coming to Canada and building a new life. He discusses the challenges of cultural adjustment, language barriers, and facing Islamophobia in his new community. Despite these obstacles, Ahmed actively engages in community organizations, advocates for interfaith

dialogue, and works to dispel stereotypes about Muslims. Ahmed's journey to Canada was not easy. As a Muslim immigrant, he faced language barriers, cultural adjustment, and the daunting task of building a new life in a foreign country. On top of that, he faced Islamophobia in his new community, with strangers assuming he was a terrorist or a threat to national security. Despite these obstacles, Ahmed refused to let fear and hatred define his experience. He actively engaged in community organizations, advocated for interfaith dialogue, and worked to dispel stereotypes about Muslims. His journey was not easy, but his resilience and commitment to fostering understanding and inclusion make him a true inspiration.

3. Fatima's Fight for Justice: Fatima, a Canadian Muslim activist, shares her experience of advocating for justice after her son became a victim of a hate crime. She narrates the initial shock and pain of the incident, but also highlights her determination to seek justice and hold the perpetrators accountable. Fatima's world turned upside down when her son became a victim of a hate crime. The pain and trauma of the incident were overwhelming, but she refused to let her son's attackers go unpunished. Fatima became a fierce advocate for justice, speaking out against

Islamophobia and pushing for accountability from those responsible. Her resilience and strength through this traumatic experience were awe-inspiring. Fatima reminds us of the importance of standing up to hate and fighting for a just society. Fatima's story sheds light on the resilience and strength of individuals who refuse to let Islamophobia go unchallenged and strive for a more just society.

4. Mohammad's Academic Journey: Mohammad, a Muslim student pursuing higher education, shares his experience of facing discrimination on campus. He discusses instances of Islamophobic remarks from peers, professors, and even administrators.

Mohammad walks into his university every day, bracing himself for the Islamophobic remarks he knows he will face from peers and even professors. Despite this constant barrage of discrimination, he refuses to let it dampen his spirit or his academic journey. Mohammad becomes an active member of student organizations that promote diversity and inclusivity. He uses his platform to educate others about Islam and challenge stereotypes. Through his advocacy and activism, Mohammad shows us the power of resilience and the importance of actively working towards a more inclusive and accepting society.

These personal stories are just a few examples of the challenges and struggles faced by Canadian Muslims in a society still grappling with systemic Islamophobia. Despite the adversity they face, these individuals refuse to let discrimination and hate define their experiences. Their resilience and determination to build a better, more inclusive Canada is an inspiration to us all.

The impact of Islamophobia on Canadian Muslim communities

Islamophobia has had a significant impact on Muslim communities in Canada. These communities have faced discrimination, exclusion, and even violence due to negative stereotypes and harmful attitudes towards

Islam and Muslims. This has led to a range of social, economic, and psychological challenges that have affected individuals and the community as a whole.

One of the most significant impacts of Islamophobia has been the social exclusion of Muslim communities. Muslims have been portrayed as outsiders and even enemies of the Canadian state, leading to a sense of isolation and marginalization. This has made it difficult for Muslim Canadians to fully participate in society and feel like they belong. It has also led to a rise in hate crimes and discrimination, which have a ripple effect on the community as a whole.

Economically, Islamophobic policies and attitudes have also had a significant impact on Muslim communities. Muslims have faced employment discrimination, resulting in limited access to jobs and opportunities for career advancement. This has led to economic disparities and an inability to fully contribute to the economy. Islamophobia has also affected the business sector, with Muslim-owned businesses facing discrimination and loss of revenue due to negative stereotypes.

The psychological impact of Islamophobia on Canadian Muslim communities cannot be understated. The constant fear of being targeted or attacked, the stress of having to prove one's loyalty and patriotism, and the feeling of being constantly watched and surveilled takes a toll on individuals' mental health. Studies have shown that Muslim

Canadians experience high levels of anxiety, depression, and post-traumatic stress disorder due to Islamophobia.

Moreover, the increased surveillance and racial profiling of Muslim communities has further perpetuated Islamophobia, leading to a sense of injustice and mistrust towards the Canadian government. The feeling of being singled out and targeted by the government has eroded trust and confidence in Canadian democracy.

The impact of Islamophobia on Canadian Muslim communities is significant and far-reaching. It affects individuals, families, and the community as a whole. It is essential for Canadian society to recognize and address the harmful effects of Islamophobia to ensure that all members of society feel included and valued.

Strategies for challenging systemic Islamophobia and promoting inclusion

Challenging systemic Islamophobia and promoting inclusion requires a multi-faceted approach that involves individuals, communities, institutions, and the government. Here are some strategies to address systemic Islamophobia and promote inclusion in Canadian society:

1. Education and awareness: Promote education and awareness programs that provide accurate information about Islam and Muslims, dispel stereotypes,

and foster understanding. This can include initiatives in schools, workplaces, and community centers, as well as media campaigns that challenge Islamophobic narratives.

2. Community engagement: Foster dialogue and collaboration between Muslim communities and other segments of society. Encourage interfaith and intercultural initiatives that promote understanding, respect, and solidarity. This can include community events, workshops, and initiatives that bring people from different backgrounds together.

3. Government policies and legislation: Advocate for government policies and

legislation that address discrimination and promote inclusion. This can involve advocating for strong anti-discrimination laws, measures to combat hate crimes, and policies that promote diversity and equal representation in various sectors.

4. Empowering Muslim voices: Ensure the representation and participation of Muslims in decision-making processes, institutions, and media. Support initiatives that amplify Muslim voices and perspectives, such as promoting Muslim leadership, providing platforms for diverse Muslim voices in media, and engaging Muslims in policy development.

5. Counteracting media bias: Encourage media outlets to provide fair and accurate coverage of Islam and Muslims. Promote media literacy and critical thinking skills to challenge Islamophobic narratives. Support media organizations that prioritize diversity and provide accurate representation of Muslim communities.

6. Allyship and solidarity: Encourage individuals and communities to be active allies in challenging Islamophobia. Promote intercommunity partnerships, support initiatives led by Muslim organizations, and advocate for inclusive policies and practices in various spheres of society.

7. Addressing systemic inequities: Recognize and address systemic inequities that contribute to Islamophobia. This includes addressing issues such as employment discrimination, unequal access to education and healthcare, and socioeconomic disparities that disproportionately affect Muslim communities.

8. Engaging with policymakers: Engage with policymakers at various levels of government to advocate for policies and programs that address systemic Islamophobia. This can involve meeting with elected officials, participating in public consultations,

and supporting organizations that work on policy advocacy.

9. Building coalitions: Collaborate with other communities and organizations working towards social justice and inclusion. By forming coalitions and alliances, collective efforts can be strengthened, amplifying the voices and impact of those challenging Islamophobia.

10. Continual self-reflection: Individuals and communities should engage in self-reflection and critically examine their own biases and prejudices. This involves challenging personal assumptions, stereotypes, and

preconceptions about Islam and Muslims.

Addressing systemic Islamophobia and promoting inclusion is an ongoing process that requires long-term commitment and collective action. By implementing these strategies, Canadian society can work towards a more inclusive, equitable, and harmonious future for all its members.

Chapter 6: Moving Forward

The need for a comprehensive strategy to combat Islamophobia

The need for a comprehensive strategy to combat Islamophobia is crucial in addressing the complex and systemic nature of this issue. A piecemeal approach is insufficient to tackle the deep-rooted biases, discriminatory practices, and negative attitudes that perpetuate Islamophobia. Here are some key reasons why a comprehensive strategy is necessary:

1. Systemic nature of Islamophobia: Islamophobia is not limited to individual prejudices or isolated incidents; it is embedded within

systems, institutions, and policies. A comprehensive strategy recognizes this systemic nature and aims to address the underlying structural factors that contribute to Islamophobia.

2. Intersectionality: Islamophobia intersects with other forms of discrimination, such as racism, xenophobia, and sexism. A comprehensive strategy acknowledges these intersecting dimensions and works towards creating an inclusive society that addresses multiple forms of discrimination and marginalization.

3. Multi-level approach: Islamophobia exists at individual, community, institutional, and societal levels. A

comprehensive strategy addresses all these levels and recognizes that effective change requires interventions at each level. It involves engaging individuals, empowering communities, challenging institutional biases, and fostering societal understanding and acceptance.

4. Holistic solutions: Islamophobia affects various aspects of life, including education, employment, housing, and public discourse. A comprehensive strategy employs a holistic approach, seeking to create inclusive policies, promote diversity in all sectors, improve access to resources and opportunities, and challenge

discriminatory practices across different domains.

5. Long-term impact: Addressing Islamophobia requires sustained effort and a long-term commitment. A comprehensive strategy provides a roadmap for long-term change, including ongoing education and awareness programs, policy reform, and regular evaluation and monitoring of progress.

6. Collaboration and coordination: A comprehensive strategy encourages collaboration and coordination among various stakeholders, including government agencies, community organizations, educational institutions,

media outlets, and advocacy groups. By working together, these stakeholders can leverage their resources, expertise, and influence to create a collective impact.

7. Empowering affected communities: A comprehensive strategy places a strong emphasis on empowering affected communities to become agents of change. It involves creating spaces for community voices to be heard, supporting community-led initiatives, and providing resources and capacity-building opportunities for affected individuals and organizations.

8. Preventive measures: In addition to addressing existing Islamophobia, a

comprehensive strategy focuses on preventive measures. This includes promoting inclusive education, fostering intercultural understanding from an early age, and implementing policies that proactively challenge discrimination and promote inclusivity.

By adopting a comprehensive strategy to combat Islamophobia, societies can work towards creating an environment that is respectful, inclusive, and free from discrimination. Such a strategy acknowledges the complex nature of Islamophobia and provides a framework for sustained action to bring about positive change at multiple levels of society.

The role of individuals, communities, and government in promoting inclusion

The role of individuals, communities, and government is crucial in promoting inclusion and combating Islamophobia. Each of these stakeholders has a unique role to play in creating an inclusive society that values diversity and promotes equality.

Individuals can play a significant role in challenging Islamophobia by:

1. Educating themselves about Islam and Muslim culture to dispel myths and stereotypes.

2. Challenging and speaking out against Islamophobic attitudes and behaviors when they witness them.

3. Engaging in dialogue and building relationships with Muslim individuals and communities to foster understanding and empathy.

4. Supporting advocacy and community initiatives that challenge Islamophobia and promote inclusivity.

5. Reflecting on their own biases and prejudices and working towards addressing them.

Communities can also play a vital role in promoting inclusion and combating Islamophobia by:

1. Building inclusive spaces that welcome and value diversity.

2. Creating opportunities for interfaith and intercultural dialogue and collaboration.

3. Supporting community-led initiatives that challenge Islamophobia and promote inclusivity.

4. Fostering a sense of belonging and identity for Muslim individuals and communities.

5. Working towards building alliances with other communities affected by discrimination and marginalization.

The government also has a crucial role to play in promoting inclusion and combating Islamophobia by:

1. Implementing policies and programs that promote inclusivity and address systemic barriers to equality.

2. Enforcing anti-discrimination laws and challenging Islamophobic practices and policies.

3. Supporting community-led initiatives and engaging with affected

communities to ensure their voices are heard.

4. Providing resources and funding for education, awareness-raising, and capacity-building initiatives that challenge Islamophobia.

5. Working towards creating a diverse and representative workforce that reflects the population it serves.

By recognizing the unique roles of individuals, communities, and government in promoting inclusion and challenging Islamophobia, stakeholders can work together to create a more inclusive and respectful society. Such collaborative efforts can lead to positive change at multiple levels, including individual attitudes and behaviors, community practices and policies, and government laws and regulations.

Steps towards building a more just and inclusive Canada

Building a more just and inclusive Canada requires collective efforts from individuals, communities, and government. Here are some steps that can be taken towards this goal:

1. Education: Education is key to challenging Islamophobia and promoting inclusivity. This includes educating oneself and others about

Islam, Muslim culture, and the impact of discrimination and marginalization.

2. Dialogue: Engaging in dialogue and building relationships between individuals and communities can help foster understanding, empathy, and respect.

Advocacy: Supporting and engaging in advocacy initiatives that challenge Islamophobia and promote inclusivity can help create a more just and inclusive society.

3. Diversity and representation: Encouraging diversity and representation in all aspects of society, including government, media, and

business, can help create a society that values and celebrates diversity.

4. Anti-discrimination policies and laws: Ensuring that anti-discrimination policies and laws are enforced and challenging discriminatory practices and policies can help address systemic barriers to equality.

5. Inclusive spaces: Creating inclusive spaces, including schools, workplaces, and public spaces, can help foster a sense of belonging and identity for marginalized communities.

6. Support for marginalized communities: Providing resources and support for marginalized communities, including

Muslim communities, can help address the impact of discrimination and marginalization.

7. Intersectionality: Recognizing the intersectionality of discrimination and working towards creating an inclusive society that addresses multiple forms of discrimination and marginalization.

8. Collaboration: Working collaboratively across sectors and with affected communities can help create a more effective and impactful approach towards addressing systemic issues of discrimination and marginalization.

By taking these steps towards building a more just and inclusive Canada, we can work towards creating a society that values and celebrates diversity, promotes equality, and challenges discrimination and marginalization in all its forms.

Conclusion

Systemic Islamophobia is a pervasive issue in Canadian society that has significant impacts on the lives of Canadian Muslims. This book has explored the historical context of Islamophobia in Canada, the impact of events such as 9/11 and the War on Terror, the role of media and politics in perpetuating Islamophobia, and the various ways that discrimination and marginalization affect Canadian Muslims.

However, this book has also highlighted the resilience and strength of Canadian Muslim communities in the face of discrimination and marginalization. Personal stories of discrimination and resilience demonstrate the impact of systemic Islamophobia on individuals and communities, and the strategies for challenging Islamophobia and promoting inclusion provide a roadmap for building a more just and inclusive society.

It is clear that addressing systemic Islamophobia requires collective action from individuals, communities, and government. It is incumbent upon all Canadians to challenge Islamophobia, promote inclusion, and work towards building a society that values and celebrates diversity. Only then can we create a more just and equitable Canada for all.

The importance of recognizing the true cost of hate

The true cost of hate is immeasurable. When we allow hatred to go unchecked, it creates a ripple effect throughout our communities. The financial cost of hate crimes, lost economic potential, and increased security measures is staggering. However, the human cost of hate is even more significant. Hate creates a culture of fear and mistrust, where individuals and communities feel isolated and marginalized. It creates barriers to education, employment, and other opportunities, limiting the potential of those who are targeted.

In the case of systemic Islamophobia, recognizing the true cost is particularly important. This form of discrimination is often invisible to those who do not experience it firsthand, and as a result, it can be challenging to quantify its impact. However, by understanding the extent of the problem, we can begin to take concrete steps towards addressing it. This includes challenging harmful stereotypes and biases, promoting inclusion and diversity, and holding those who perpetuate hate accountable.

Recognizing the true cost of hate also means acknowledging the lived experiences of those who are impacted by it. By listening to and centering the experiences of Canadian Muslims, we can better understand the impact of systemic Islamophobia and work towards creating a more just and equitable society for all. Ultimately, it is only by recognizing and addressing the true cost of hate that we can build a more inclusive and compassionate Canada for future generations.

A call to action for all Canadians.

The pervasive issue of systemic Islamophobia in Canada demands a call to action from all Canadians. It is incumbent upon us all to recognize the harm and discrimination faced by Canadian Muslims and to work towards building a more just and inclusive society.

As individuals, we can challenge Islamophobia and other forms of hate by educating ourselves about these issues, calling out discriminatory attitudes and behaviors, and showing solidarity with those affected by hate. We can also support organizations and initiatives that promote inclusion and work towards creating a more equitable society.

As communities, we can come together to promote dialogue, understanding, and respect between different cultural and religious groups. We can work towards building bridges across communities, fostering empathy and compassion, and creating safe spaces where everyone can feel valued and respected.

As government, there is a responsibility to create policies and programs that promote inclusion, challenge discrimination, and protect the rights of all Canadians. This includes investing in education and awareness campaigns, supporting initiatives that promote diversity and inclusion, and ensuring that hate crimes are vigorously prosecuted.

In conclusion, we must all play a role in combating systemic Islamophobia and promoting inclusion in Canada. By working together and standing up against hate in all its forms, we can build a more just and equitable society, where everyone can feel valued, respected, and included.